EVERY
ONE

It takes each of us
to make a difference
for all of us.

LEADS

Compiled by Dan Zadra
Designed by Kobi Yamada and Steve Potter

COMPENDIUM™
PUBLISHING

live inspired.

ACKNOWLEDGEMENTS

These quotations were gathered lovingly but unscientifically over several years and/or contributed by many friends or acquaintances. Some arrived—and survived in our files—on scraps of paper and may therefore be imperfectly worded or attributed. To the authors, contributors and original sources, our thanks, and where appropriate, our apologies. —The editors

WITH SPECIAL THANKS TO

Jason Aldrich, Gerry Baird, Jay Baird, Neil Beaton, Doug Cruickshank, Jim Darragh, Jennifer & Matt Ellison, Josie & Rob Estes, Michael Flynn, Jennifer Hurwitz, Liam Lavery, Connie McMartin, Cristal & Brad Olberg, Janet Potter & Family, Aimee Rawlins, Diane Roger, Jenica Wilkie, Heidi & Shale Yamada, Justi, Tote & Caden Yamada, Robert & Val Yamada, Kaz, Kristin, Kyle & Kendyl Yamada, Tai & Joy Yamada, Anne Zadra, August & Arline Zadra.

CREDITS

Compiled by Dan Zadra
Designed by Kobi Yamada and Steve Potter

Printed in Hong Kong

CONTENTS

A Better Way to Fly

There was a time when the lone eagle on the mountain was a popular symbol for leadership. But today's fast-moving organization should have—must have—leaders at every position. If you want a better metaphor than the eagle, consider the wild and wily Great Northern Geese.

Everyone is aligned: A flock of Great Northern Geese will fly thousands of miles in a perfect V formation—and therein lies the secret: As each bird moves its great wings, it creates an uplift for the bird following. Formation flying is 70 percent more efficient than flying alone.

Everyone leads: At a distance, the flock appears to be guided by a single leader. The lead bird does in fact guide the formation, winging smoothly and confidently through the oncoming elements. If the lead bird tires, however, it rotates back into formation and another bird moves quickly to the point position. Leadership is willingly shared, and each bird knows exactly where the entire group is headed.

Everyone inspires: Each flock finds its own unique rhythm and spirit. The pulsating sound of the huge wings beating together excites and energizes the entire formation. The geese enthusiastically honk from behind to encourage those up front to keep up with their speed.

Everyone cares: In good times or bad, Great Northern Geese stand by each other. When a member of the flock gets sick, wounded or shot down, two geese drop out of formation and follow it down to help and protect it. They stay with it until it is able to fly again. Then they soar off together to catch up with their flock.

If we have as much sense as geese, we too will share the leadership and stand by each other in difficult times as well as when we are strong.

Dan Zadra

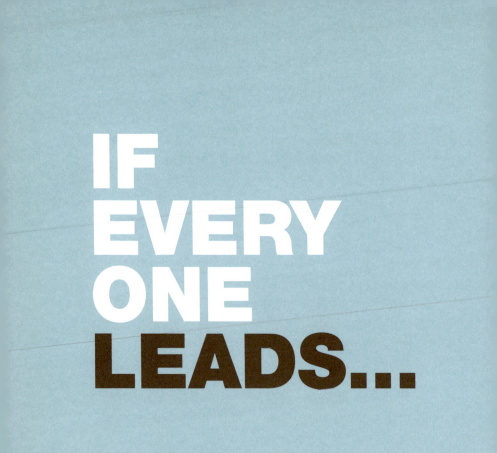

IF EVERY ONE LEADS...

I start with the premise that the function of leadership is to produce more leaders, not more followers.

—RALPH NADER

Good leaders surround themselves with good people, who in turn become good leaders.

—MICHAEL NOLAN

The times do not allow anyone the luxury of waiting around for others to lead. All can lead and ought to be invited to do so.

—MATTHEW FOX

What makes a company great is not primarily its top leaders, but the quality of its innumerable everyday ones.

—JOHN HOLMES

The major job was getting everyone to understand and believe that they had something within their personal power to contribute—something that no one else could contribute.

—ELLA BAKER

Everyone has a purpose. You are not here by mistake.

—BEN MORROW

Leadership is contagious.

—GIL ATKINSON

Very few natural-born leaders
turn up in the workplace.
People become leaders.

—MILTON COTTER

We're not born into leadership.
We convert.

—GOOD COMPANY

Good leaders were first good followers.

—DON WARD

Organizational change begins
with leaders who walk the talk by
transforming themselves, and then invite
everyone in the organization to
lead alongside them.

—FORTUNE MAGAZINE

Leadership is not about making yourself
more powerful. It's about making people around
you more powerful.

—BETTY LINTON

The key to successful leadership today
is influence, not authority.

—KENNETH BLANCHARD

Strange as it sounds,
the best leaders gain authority
by giving it away.

—JAMES B. STOCKDALE

In a healthy organization,
rewards come by empowering others,
not by climbing over them.

—JOHN NAISBETT

Hire the best people, trust them,
and then delegate with abandon.

—FRANK VIZZARE

Every opportunity counts.
When your people come to you for leadership,
they're giving you another chance—
to help them grow into leaders themselves.

—ERIC ALLENBAUGH

True leadership is the art of changing a group from
what it is into what it ought to be. It's not something
that is done "to" people, it is something done
"with" people. By that definition, every person in your
organization can and must lead.

—JAN GREENE

Excellent organizations
do not foster "we and they" attitudes.

—TOM PETERS

The best leaders will be those
who listen to their people to figure out
where they should be going.

—JACK KAHL

I can lead, and I can follow.
An important aspect of leadership is
knowing when to do which.

—AL GARSIS

Leaders need to remember that wisdom does not solely reside in the corner office.

—DIANE BRANSON

You don't have to be in "Who's Who" to know what's what.

—SAM LEVENSON

The ultimate test for a leader is not whether he or she makes smart decisions and takes decisive action, but whether he or she teaches others to make smart decisions and take decisive action.

—NOEL M. TICHY

The hyperfast-moving, wired-up, reengineered, quality-obsessed organization will succeed or fail on the strength of the trust that its managers place in the folks working on the front line.

—TOM PETERS

Use your own best judgment at all times.

—NORDSTROM CORP.
(entire contents of $1.9 billion company's policy manual)

Victory is much more meaningful when it comes not just from one person, but from the joint achievements of many. The euphoria is lasting when all participants lead with their hearts, winning not just for themselves but for one another.

—HOWARD SCHULTZ, STARBUCKS

IF EVERY ONE BELIEVES...

Leadership is communicating the company's Vision and Mission and having the courage to follow it. Companies that endure have a noble purpose.

—JOE JAWORSKI

A business that makes nothing but money is a poor business.

—HENRY FORD

Great companies make meaning. A company has a name, but its people give it a meaning.

—RICHARD PASCALE

Leaders are people who focus attention on a vision.

—WARREN BENNIS

A clear definition of the Mission is the foundation for leadership.

—PETER DRUCKER

Your Mission statement provides the why that inspires every how.

—CHARLES GARFIELD

There's more to life than simply crossing things off our To-Do list.

—JAY MANES

If all anyone takes home from their job is a paycheck, then they take home too little.

—GLENDON JOHNSON

Each of us wants to be treated as a unique and valuable individual, but we each have a simultaneous need to belong to something greater than ourselves, something more than one alone can do or be.

—BUILDING COMMUNITY

Organizations exist only for one purpose: to help people reach a higher purpose together—something wonderful that they couldn't achieve individually.

—ROBERT H. WATERMAN

Part of true success is understanding that there's something bigger and more important than ourselves.

—MARCIA ANN GILLESPIE

If people relate to the company they work for, if they form an emotional tie to it and buy into its dreams, they will pour their heart into making it better.

—HOWARD SCHULTZ, STARBUCKS

Ninety percent of leadership
is the ability to communicate something
people either want, or want to achieve.

—DIANE FEINSTEIN

It is not enough to be industrious;
so are the ants. What are we industrious about?

—HENRY DAVID THOREAU

True loyalty doesn't come through
money or coercion, it comes through shared
meaning and commitment.

—DAN ZADRA

The shortest distance
between two points is an intention.

—BENJAMIN SHIELD, PH.D.

If you want to attract the best
and the brightest, then you have to build
an organization you feel good about—one that has
a clear and meaningful purpose in the world.

—WILLIAM C. FORD, JR.

Once your organization has articulated
a clear and compelling Vision of the future…
once everyone believes in the Vision and is
committed to attaining it…then all sorts of unforeseen
assistance will rush in magically to support you.

—DON WARD

A vague desire isn't a Mission, it's a dream.

—RHONDA ABRAMS

Make the Mission and Vision clear
and tangible by sharing it with others.
Say it out loud and put it on paper. Often.

—RHONDA ABRAMS

A Mission unbelieved is always
considered nonsense. But a Mission believed
is history in the making.

—JIM WALLIS

Superior work teams recognize that consistently high performance can be built not on rules but only on values.

—DENNIS KINLAW

Responsibility begins with a dream of something greater than ourselves. Enthusiasm and energy are equal to desire and purpose.

—EVA SIKARSKI

Our greatest strength comes not from what we possess, but from what we believe; not from what we have, but from who we are.

—MICHAEL DUKAKIS

Ultimately there can be no success or happiness if the things we believe in are different from the things we do.

—FREYA MADELINE STARK

When we're in our nineties and we're looking back, it's not going to be how much money we made or how many awards we've won. It's really "What did we stand for? Did we make a positive difference for people?"

—ELIZABETH DOLE

Tomorrow, who will really care how fast we grew? Isn't it more important to know what we are building with our growth, and why? Measuring more is easy; measuring better is hard. Measuring better requires a clear mission, an exciting vision and shared values.

—RON KENDRICK

IF
EVERY
ONE
COMMITS....

Never mistake a clear view for a short distance.

—MARK SPAIN

If all difficulties were known at
the onset of a long journey, most of
us would never start out at all.

—DAN RATHER

Change takes guts.
It takes imagination. It takes commitment.

—JOHN TAYLOR

All of us must learn this lesson somewhere—
that it costs something to be what we are.

—SHIRLEY ABBOTT

The cost of a thing is the amount
of what I call life which is required to
be exchanged for it, immediately
or in the long run.

—HENRY DAVID THOREAU

Whenever I get to a low point,
I go back to the basics. I ask myself,
"Why am I doing this?"
It comes down to passion.

—LYN ST. JAMES

When the crunch comes, people cling to those they know they can trust—those who are not detached, but involved.

—ADMIRAL JAMES STOCKDALE

You may trod me into the very dirt but still, like dust, I'll rise.

—MAYA ANGELOU

Commitment! We're talking the heavy, deep, man/woman on a mission stuff. When the grenades are flying, the committed person doesn't go AWOL. There is nothing more powerful than emotional equity. No amount of stock options even comes close.

—CHRISTINE COMAFORD

29

These are the hard times in which a genius would wish to live. Great necessities call forth great leaders.

—ABIGAIL ADAMS

Wherever we look upon this earth, the opportunities take shape within the problems.

—NELSON A. ROCKEFELLER

We have a problem. "Congratulations." But it's a tough problem. "Then double congratulations."

—W. CLEMENT STONE

Out of difficulties we grow miracles.

—JEAN DE LA BRUYERE

A good business has interesting problems;
a bad business has boring ones. The idea is to
make the problems so interesting that everyone
wants to get to work and deal with them.

—SUSAN FIELDER

There is nothing we cannot live down,
rise above or overcome.

—ELLA WHEELER-WILCOX

Don't make excuses—make good.

—ELBERT HUBBARD

We must exchange the philosophy of excuses—
what I am is beyond my control—
for the philosophy of responsibility.

—BARBARA JORDAN

Leadership, pure and simple,
is the assumption of responsibility for the
pursuit of excellence in group life.

—PHILIP SELZNICK

Those who enjoy responsibility usually get it; those who merely like exercising authority usually lose it.

—MALCOLM FORBES

It is commitment, not authority, that produces results.

—WILLIAM GORE

It's easier to say what we believe than be what we believe.

—DR. ROBERT ANTHONY

Leaders always pick themselves up after defeat.

—DAVID OGILVY

Vitality shows not only in the ability to persist, but in the ability to start over.

—F. SCOTT FITZGERALD

Ever tried. Ever failed. No matter. Try again. Fail again. Fail better.

—SAMUEL BECKETT

Sticking to it is the genius.

—THOMAS EDISON

Show up and keep showing up.
One day you'll look up and
you'll be in front of the line.

—TOM COLEMAN

Commitment to each other is critical.
Let's make our deadlines and due dates mean something.
For changes to occur, we have to embrace them over
and over. Take it step by step—but keep moving
forward—and a year from now, we'll find we've
moved from here to there.

—RHONDA ABRAMS

IF EVERY ONE CARES...

It's time to start thinking with the heart.

—BEVERLEY WILSON

Leaders have passion
and are willing to show it.

—SANDY LINVER

I believe with all my heart in what we do.
It is contagious with people. They want that kind
of leadership, and they want to give it too.

—GERALD ANDERSON

The one piece of advice which will contribute to making you a better leader, will provide you with greater happiness and will advance your career more than any other advice…and it doesn't call for a special personality or any certain chemistry…and anyone can do it, and it's this: You must care.

—LT. GENERAL MELVIN ZAIS

Commit to your job and your work, whatever it is. Believe in it more than anything else. If you love your work, you'll be out there every day trying to do the best you can, and pretty soon everybody around will catch the passion from you.

—SAM WALTON

Caring is the ultimate competitive advantage.

—RON KENDRICK

We could hardly wait
to get up in the morning.

—WILBUR WRIGHT

The success or failure of any company boils down
to one question: Are you operating from passion?
If you are, you're going to succeed. If you believe
in what you're doing, you're going to make sure that
everyone around you believes in it too.

—MAGGIE HUGHES

Leaders focus on emotional issues
that connect them with their team.

—JOHN ZENGER

The country is full of good coaches.
What it takes to win is a bunch of interested players.

—DON CORYELL

One person who wants something is
a hundred times stronger than a hundred who
want to be left alone.

—BARBARA WARD

Bet on people, not strategies.

—LARRY BOSSIDY

If we want someone to do a good job,
we must give them a good job to do.

—FREDERICK HERZBERG

Search for ways to give
every employee more control over his or
her piece of the business.

—BOB GILBERTSON

Leadership is a state of mind and
a way of life, not something that one turns on or off.

—STEVE ADAMS

The passion to make and make again.

—ADRIENNE RICH

I went back to being an amateur,
in the sense of somebody who loves what she is doing.
If a professional loses the love of work, routine sets in,
and that's the death of work and life.

—ADA BETHUNE

Example is leadership.

—ALBERT SCHWEITZER

A leader is anyone people emulate.
Leadership is knowing you are emulated,
enthusiastically embracing that role, and behaving
in a defined way to reach a common goal.

—STEVEN WHITAKER

If you set the right example,
you won't need to worry about the rules.

—GAR WRIGHT

Commitment is never an act of moderation.

—KENNETH G. MILLS

I want to work with people who feel intensely alive.
I'd rather have them against me than indifferent.

—MARTHA GRAHAM

Ye gads, wake up! Breathe!
Go down swinging. Try something. Try anything.
Be A-L-I-V-E, for heaven's sake!

—TOM PETERS

I feel sorry for the person who
can't get genuinely excited about his work.
Not only will he never be satisfied, but he will
never achieve anything worthwhile.

—WALTER CHRYSLER

I don't believe people are looking for
the meaning of life as much as they are
looking for the experience of being alive.

—JOSEPH CAMPBELL

That is happiness; to be dissolved
into something complete and great.

—WILLA CATHER

IF EVERY ONE DARES...

Leadership begins when you get out of the grandstands and into the game.

—P.L. DEBEVOISE

Imagine if everyone in the company had the courage and the confidence and the risk-seeking profile that we associate with leaders. That's the direction every company must head.

—CHANCE DUNCAN

Do something. Either lead, follow, or get out of the way.

—TED TURNER

Leadership is action, not position.

—DONALD H. MCGANNON

Effective leaders work throughout
the organization; they do not just sit on top.

—H. MINTZBERG

You cannot lead where you do not go.

—DON WARD

I don't believe in ordering people to do things. You have to sort of grab an oar and row with them.

—HAROLD GENEEN

Do-so is more important than say-so.

—PETE SEEGER

There's a big difference between seeing an opportunity and seizing an opportunity.

—JIM MOORE

There is nothing more genuine than breaking away from the chorus to learn the sound of your own voice.

—P.O. BRANSON

Leading is to claim the power of your freedom, your essence as a self-starter.

—PETER KOESTENBAUM

Sometimes if you want to see a change for the better, you have to take things into your own hands.

—CLINT EASTWOOD

The perfect bureaucrat somehow manages to make no decisions and escapes all responsibility.

—BROOKS ATKINSON

Master Leadership Principle:
Put your butt on the line.

—FRANK VIZZARE

Those who are willing to accept responsibility usually get it. That's how true leaders are born.

—DON WARD

Not all birds can fly.
What separates the flyers from
the walkers is the ability to take off.

—CARL SAGAN

I am always doing things I can't do—
that's how I get to do them.

—PABLO PICASSO

It's not that hard, really.
Just look for your choices, pick the best one,
go with it—and then stand by it.

—PAT RILEY

Leaders act decisively in the absence of certainty.

—BERTRAND RUSSELL

Problems are solved on the spot, as soon as they arise. No frontline employee should ever have to wait for a supervisor's permission.

—JAN CARLZON

We can do anything in this world if we are prepared to take the consequences.

—W. SOMERSET MAUGHAM

Why is there such a huge difference between "said" and "done"?

—FRANK VIZZARE

Change starts when someone sees the next step.

—WILLIAM DRAYTON

I see something that has to be done and I organize it.

—ELINOR GUGGENHEIMER

Let's not just talk about our company values, let's put them into action. Let's not just memorize them, let's live them.

—RON KENDRICK

All of us can take steps—no matter how small and insignificant at the start—in the direction we want to go.

—MARSHA SINETAR

The more we overcome our reluctance and take action, the more we realize just how often things can go well for us.

—CATERINA RANDO

IF
EVERY
ONE
IMAGINES...

We have enough people who tell it like it is—
now we could use a few who tell it like it can be.

—ROBERT ORBEN

The hero is the one with the ideas.

—JACK WELCH

We need more "What if?" thinkers.

—DAN ZADRA

Memo to all managers:
There will be no more long-range planning.

—HAROLD GENEEN

Change is here to stay,
and the rate of change is accelerating.
It's time to throw away those five-year plans.
Those who survive and prosper will be those who
endlessly innovate and adapt.

—DON WARD

Rule for leaders: Innovate or abdicate.
Rule for companies: Innovate or evaporate.

—BOB HEINZ

Creativity is the most effective response to rapid change.

—ROBERT PORTER LYNCH

The future is not something we enter, it's something we create.

—LEONARD I. SWEET

We are what and where we are because we have first imagined it.

—DONALD CURTIS

To find an open road, have an open mind.

—JOHN TOWNE

The need to be right all the time is the biggest barrier to new ideas.

—EDWARD DE BONO

The best leaders are not interested in selling their own ideas, but in finding the best ideas. They are not interested in having their own way, but in finding the best way.

—WILFRED PETERSON

Where you want the contest is not among people, but among ideas.

—CASEY COWELL

Innovation comes only from readily and seamlessly sharing information rather than hoarding it.

—TOM PETERS

Speak out! The ability to express an idea is well nigh as important as the idea itself.

—BERNARD BARUCH

People were born to innovate, to invent.
—MICROSOFT

We are all born originals—
why is it so many of us die copies?
—ED YOUNG

Why should only a small percentage of Americans
view themselves as creative? What has happened
to our notorious disdain for the status quo?
Our fabled pioneer spirit? Has our taste for the big idea
or breakthrough become a thing of the past?
—GREAT IDEAS

The best way to get people to think out of the box is not to create the box in the first place.

—MARTIN COOPER

It irritates me to be told how things have always been done. I defy the tyranny of precedent. I cannot afford the luxury of a closed mind. I go for anything new that might improve the past.

—CLARA BARTON

Leaders don't resist innovation, they symbolize it.

—DAVID OGILVY

The difficulty lies not so much in developing new ideas as in escaping from the old ones.

—JOHN MAYNARD KEYNES

Living in the past is a dull and lonely business; looking back strains the neck muscles, causes you to bump into people not going your way.

—EDNA FERBER

The good old days? The only good days are ahead.

—ALICE CHILDRESS

Rules are for when thinking stops.

—H. DEAN MALLORY

We will be remembered for all the rules we break.

—DOUGLAS MACARTHUR

Out beyond ideas of wrong-doing or right-doing there is an open field. I'll meet you there.

—RUMI

IF
EVERY
ONE
COLLABORATES...

It's good to remember that the entire universe,
with one minor exception, is composed of others.

—JOHN ANDREW HOLMES

You can do anything—
but you can't do everything.

—DAVID ALLEN

One determined person
can make a significant difference,
but a small group of determined people can
change the course of history.

—SONIA JOHNSON

67

Excellence is not a spectator sport.
Everyone's involved.

—GENERAL ELECTRIC

Cooperation is everything.
The organization is just the vehicle
for human cooperation.

—FRANCIS GOUILLART

Strategy is not something that's done in a box
by one person with only a rational hat on. It needs to
be visceral, human, and often emotional—
and everyone must be involved in creating it.

—ROBERT STONE

As a rule of thumb, involve everyone in everything of any consequence to all of you.

—TOM PETERS

Tell them quick, tell them often.

—WILLIAM WRIGLEY, JR.

Communicate everything you possibly can to your partners and teammates. The more they understand, the more they'll care. Once they care, there's no stopping them.

—SAM WALTON

People can't answer a call that isn't made.

—ROBERT MORGAN

An individual without information
cannot take responsibility; an individual who is given
information cannot help but take responsibility.

—JAN CARLZON

Information isn't power. It's a burden.
Share information, and you share the
burdens of leadership as well.

—JACK STACK

If you don't like bad news, you should get out of the leadership business. Your job is to hear as much bad news as there is out there and to figure out ways of dealing with it.

—KIM CAMPBELL

The worse the news, the faster you should tell people.

—JAMES FALOUDI

There are no problems we cannot solve together, and very few we can solve by ourselves.

—LYNDON B. JOHNSON

There is a big difference between information and inspiration.

—SUSAN FIELDER

People look to you for heat, as well as light.

—DAN ZADRA

When the term "community" is used, the notion that typically comes to mind is a place in which people know and care for one another—the kind of place in which people do not merely ask "How are you?" as a formality, but care about the answer.

—AMITAI ETZIONI

Draw strength from each other.

—JAMES A. RENIER

History provides abundant examples of people
whose greatest gift was in redeeming, inspiring,
liberating, and nurturing the gifts of others.

—SONYA RUDIKOFF

We either make ourselves miserable
or we make ourselves strong.
The amount of work is the same.

—CARLOS CASTANEDA

Being responsible sometimes
means ticking people off.

—MARIA BARTELL

Change means movement.
Movement means friction.

—SAUL ALINSKY

Good leadership involves responsibility
to the welfare of the group, which means that
some people will get angry at your actions and
decisions. It's inevitable—if you're honorable.

—COLIN POWELL

Leadership means resisting our own urge to be the brilliant one.

—DIANE BRANSON

Let people accomplish your objectives their way.

—CLARK JOHNSON

Figure out where you leave off and everybody else begins.

—GEORGE MCCABEE

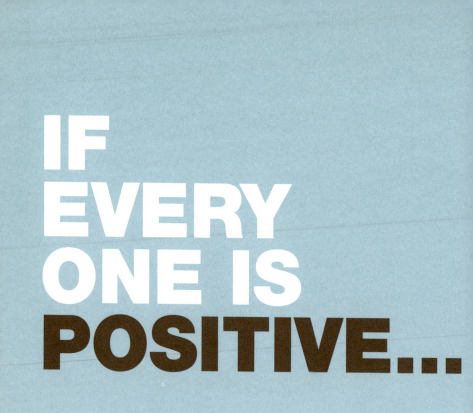

IF EVERY ONE IS POSITIVE...

Leadership is an attitude
before it becomes an ability.

—A.S. MIGS DAMIANI

It is our attitude at the beginning of
a difficult task which, more than anything else,
will affect its successful outcome.

—WILLIAM JAMES

It may be difficult, but it can be done.
That much faith is a prerequisite of any undertaking.

—MARGO JONES

The ability to envision positive outcomes
is the essence of leadership.

—DELORES AMBROSE

If you believe it will work out, you'll see opportunities.
If you believe it won't, you'll see obstacles.

—JON ALAMA

Refuse to accept the many reasons why
it can't be done and ask if there are any reasons
that it can be done.

—HANOCH MCCARTY

You can't get there from "not here."

If you want to do something, you find a way.
If you don't want to do something,
you find an excuse.

—DAWN BAUER

It shall be done—sometime,
somewhere—so, why not by you?

—OPHELIA GUYON BROWNING

Criticism comes easier than craftsmanship.

—ZEUXIS

The search for someone to blame
is always successful.

—ROBERT HALF

When we blame others,
we give up our power to change.

—DR. ROBERT ANTHONY

Drive out fear.

—DR. W. EDWARDS DEMING

Make finding a solution a
higher priority than placing blame.

—CATHY HARRINGTON

We're not trying to
point fingers—just get it right.

—GREAT IDEAS

You have to be an adult to work here.

—MARLENE SOLOMON

This is a world of action, and not for moping and groaning in.

—CHARLES DICKENS

If you can't add to the discussion, don't subtract from it.

—DENNIS CRIMP

When you bring a problem, bring a solution.

—SUSAN FIELDER

Shelving hard decisions
is the least ethical course.

—ADRIAN CADBURY

What you can't get out of,
get into wholeheartedly.

—MIGNON MCLAUGLIN

Pessimism bounces.

—LARS GREY

If you don't like what you're getting back in life, take a look at what you're putting out.

—PAMELA DREYER

Attitudes are contagious. Would anyone want to catch yours?

—BOB MOAWAD

Life is a crisis—so what?!

—MALCOLM BRADBURY

Welcome frustration.
It is a gift that signals we need
to change something.

—SUSAN FIELDER

If you don't like something,
you change it. If you can't change it,
change your attitude. Don't complain.

—MAYA ANGELOU

IF EVERY ONE ONE SERVES...

Nothing liberates our greatness like the desire to help, the desire to serve.

—MARIANNE WILLIAMSON

Who has not served cannot command.

—JOHN FLORIO

What does it mean to be promoted into a leadership position? Frankly, it means we now have the authority to serve people in a special way.

—DON WARD

Leadership is not a trumpet call to self-importance—it is an opportunity to serve.

—MEL WALLACE

The leader is the servant who removes the obstacles that prevent people from doing their jobs.

—MAX DEPREE

The good leader carries water for his people.

—LAO TZU

If he works for you, you work for him.

—JAPANESE PROVERB

We're all working together,
all taking turns serving each other—
that's the secret.

—SAM WALTON

It's a simple, predictable human chain of events:
If the company takes good care of its employees, the
employees will take good care of their customers,
and the customers will take good care of the company.

—DAN ZADRA

As individuals we are all service people.
Unless we are blood donors—then we are
manufacturing plants.

—PHILIP B. CROSBY

Everyone has an opportunity to be great
because everyone has an opportunity to serve.

—MARTIN LUTHER KING, JR.

If you're not serving the customer,
you'd better be serving someone who is.

—PHILIP B. CROSBY

To your customer's way of thinking,
you *are* the company.

—RON ZEMKE

All of us are the company,
and each of us must be committed to
providing superior value and personalized
service every single time to our customers.

—FRANK VIZZARE

Visualize every single person in your
organization as a caring, highly-motivated,
proactive, value-driven leader in sales and service.
When that comes to pass in your company,
you will be unstoppable.

—DAN ZADRA

By now, we have all figured out that the man who writes the advertisements for the bank is not the same guy who makes the loans.

—PETER'S ALMANAC

"Customer First" means that our people are empowered to go ahead and do what is right for the customer—without worry of repercussion.

—SHAUN CLARK

Eliminate bureaucracy.
Empower your employees.
Accommodate your customers.
No exceptions, no excuses.

—JIM WILLIAMSON, LESSONS LEARNED

I want that hotel reservation person to
        quit acting like a "reservation person,"
   I want him or her to be Chairman, Founder, and
CEO of Customer Care for ANYBODY who calls.

—TOM PETERS

There is no such thing as an unimportant person,
job or contact with the customer. If one employee
wows the customer now and then, that's commendable.
   But if every single employee makes an effort
   to wow the customer every single time, that's a
sales and service revolution.

—RON KENDRICK

The Law of Accumulation: The sum total
of a lot of little things isn't little.

—MICHAEL NOLAN

Would you do business with you?

—LINDA SILVERMAN GOLDZIMER

Listen closely and your customers will explain your business to you.

—PETER SCHUTZ

First and foremost and in everything you do daily, ask: "If I were the customer, would I buy it? If I were the customer, would the service I provided fulfill my expectations?"

—MARK PINNETTI

The essential difference in service
is not machines or things. The essential difference
is minds, hearts, spirits and souls.

—HERB KELLEHER, SOUTHWEST AIRLINES

Catch people in the act of
extraordinary service. Treat them like heroes.
Tell their stories, far and wide.

—SUZANNE HOONAN

Blue ribbon sales and service people are
easily one your company's greatest assets.
Honor them. Celebrate them. Reward them.

—JIM WILLIAMSON, LESSONS LEARNED

IF
EVERY
ONE
GROWS...

The future belongs to those who learn new things the fastest.

—PAUL ZANE PILZER

There has been an alarming increase in the number of things we know nothing about.

—SCIENTIFIC AMERICAN

Leadership is less about what we know and more about what we're willing to discover.

—DIANE BRANSON

Of all human resources,
the most precious is the desire
to learn and grow.

—FRANK VIZZARE

Learning is not compulsory,
but neither is survival.

—W. EDWARDS DEMING

We cannot become what we want to be
by remaining what we are.

—MAX DEPREE

For things to change, we must change.
For things to get better, we must get better.

—HEIDI WILLS

Everyone thinks of changing the world,
but no one thinks of changing himself.

—LEO TOLSTOY

Time invested in improving
ourselves cuts down on time wasted
in disapproving of others.

—LEONA GREEN

We're all capable of climbing
so much higher than we usually permit
ourselves to suppose.

—OCTAVIA BUTLER

One of the most important results
you can bring into the world is the full
you that you were meant to be.

—ROBERT FRITZ

People become who they are.
Even Beethoven became Beethoven.

—RANDY NEWMAN

Saying "yes" to yourself means
acknowledging what you have that's good
and working on the things that aren't.

—PATRICIA FRIPP

When it gets right down to it,
someone else may be signing your paycheck
but you are the person who fills in the amount.

—DON WARD

The difference between great and average
or lousy in any job is, mostly, having the
imagination and zeal to re-create yourself daily.

—TOM PETERS

We can do more than learn, we can teach.

—DAN ZADRA

The ultimate test for a leader
is not whether he or she makes smart decisions
and takes decisive action, but whether he or she
teaches others to be leaders.

—NOEL M. TICHY

No coach ever won a game
by what he knows; it's what his
players have learned.

—AMOS ALONZO STAGG

Leadership is not something that is done to people. Leadership is unlocking people's potential.

—BILL BRADLEY

We are closest to people when we help them grow.

—MILTON MAYEROFF

A good manager is less concerned about his own career path, and more concerned about the careers of the people who look to him for leadership.

—SHARON HULTZ

Leaders create a safe and open environment for people to make and learn from their mistakes.

—BOB MOAWAD

The chief object of education is not to learn things but to unlearn things.

—G.K. CHESTERTON

Learning should be full of ideas and opportunities, not stuffed with facts and routines.

—JOHN CONDRY

Keep growing.
The only real failure is to fail
to find out what you do best.

—BERNIE WEINER

I've gone through life believing
in the strength and competence of others—
never in my own. Now, dazzled, I discovered
that my capacities were real. It was like finding
a fortune in the lining of an old coat.

—JOAN MILLS

There is no good reason why
we should not grow and develop and
change until the last day we live.

—KAREN HORNEY

IF EVERY ONE CELEBRATES...

What was the duty of the leader if not to inspire?

—CARL MEREDITH

The leader's role is not to control
people or stay on top of things, but rather
to guide, energize and excite.

—JACK WELCH

Encourage each other to become
the best you can be. Celebrate what you
want to see more of.

—TOM PETERS

Anyone can blame;
it takes a specialist to praise.

—KONSTANTIN STANISLAVSKI

Throw the spotlight into every nook
and cranny of your company and catch people
in the act of doing things right.

—SCOTT JOHNSON

No one is going to win fame,
recognition, or advancement just
because he or she thinks it's deserved.
Someone else has to think so too.

—JOHN LUTHER

The joy of leadership is helping others succeed.

—ROGER STILSON

Appreciation can make a day—even change a life.

—MARGARET COUSINS

Create a career plan for everyone in your organization. Listen closely to their dreams, hopes, plans and ideas. Challenge them to grow and excel, and then recognize and celebrate them when they do.

—RON KENDRICK

Life at work can be cool—
and work that's cool isn't confined to
Tiger Woods, Yo-Yo Ma, or Tom Hanks.
It's available to all of us.

—TOM PETERS

Good leaders make the
workplace heroic. They are storytellers,
celebrators and legend-makers supreme.

—CARLA BARNES

People come together because
they need each other and they need to
hear victories about each other.

—BILL MILLIKEN

Recognition is a powerful leadership tool because it is appropriate for everyone in the organization.

—JOAN P. KLUBNIK

Appreciation is a wonderful thing; it makes what is excellent in others belong to us as well.

—VOLTAIRE

The great leader is not the one in the spotlight; he or she is the one leading the applause.

—COMMITMENT TO TEAMWORK

When nobody around you seems to measure up,
it's time to check your yardstick.

—BILL LEMLEY

Bury your ego. Don't be the star.
Be the star maker!

—BUD HADFIELD

You can work miracles by having faith in others.
To inspire the best in people, choose to think
and believe the best about them.

—BOB MOAWAD

Never give up on anybody.

—HUBERT H. HUMPHREY

My best friend is the one
who brings out the best in me.

—HENRY FORD

A true friend is one who supports you
when you are struggling, prods you to
personal growth, and celebrates your
successes as if they were his own.

—RICHARD EXLEY

The key is to keep company with people who uplift you, whose presence calls forth your best.

—EPICTETUS

Having fun is not a diversion from a successful life; it is the pathway to it.

—MARTHA BECK

People are going to be most creative and productive when they're doing something they're really interested in. So having fun isn't an outrageous idea at all. It's a very sensible one.

—JOHN SCULLEY

When you have confidence, you can
have a lot of fun. And when you have fun,
you can do amazing things.

—JOE NAMATH

Hire people with
a sense of humor. Adopt a playful attitude.
Be the first to laugh. Laugh with, not at.
Take your work seriously, but not yourself.

—HERB KELLEHER

If you're not enjoying the journey,
you probably won't enjoy the destination.

—JOE TYE

IF EVERY ONE WINS...

The first rule of survival is clear:
Nothing is more dangerous than yesterday's success.

—ALVIN TOFFLER

The achievement of excellence
can only occur if the organization promotes
a culture of continuous creative dissatisfaction.

—LAWRENCE MILLER

The trick for any sensible company is
to keep topping itself—so that any "stolen"
secrets are secrets to yesterday's success.

—TOM PETERS

Good enough is never good enough.

—SHARON BANTA

The most damaging phrase
in the English language is:
"It's always been done that way."

—REAR ADMIRAL GRACE HOPPER

Let's find out what everyone is doing,
and then stop everyone from doing it.

—A.P. HERBERT

I never think about why
something hasn't been done already—
but why nobody has done it right yet.

—MARCIA KILGORE

People who obsess over profits
wind up in the hole. Profit happens when
you do everything right.

—CHOUINARD

The urge for good design
is the same as the urge to go on living.
The assumption is that somewhere, hidden,
is a better way of doing things.

—HARRY BERTOIA

There is no such thing as expecting too much.

—SUSAN CHEEVER

If we're going to lead in our field, we can't be
A+ in some things and C+ in others.

—FRANK VIZZARE

Success will not lower its standard to us.
We must raise our standard to success.

—RANDALL R. MCBRIDE, JR.

It's the "little stuff" that torpedoes the big stuff.

—JERRY NILES

Between the failure and the masterpiece,
the distance is one millimeter.

—PAUL GAUGUIN

A genuine craftsman
will not cut corners on his product.
The reason isn't because duty says
he shouldn't, but because
passion says he couldn't.

—WALTER LIPPMANN

Size works against excellence.

—BILL GATES, MICROSOFT

The lure of quantity is the most dangerous of all.

—SIMONE WEIL

We have always found that people
are most productive in small teams with
tight budgets and time lines, and the freedom
to solve their own problems.

—JOHN ROLLWAGEN

Techniques don't produce quality products and service; people do. People who care, people who are treated as creatively contributing adults.

—TOM PETERS

Our people are responsible for their own product and its quality. We expect them to act like owners.

—GORDON FORWARD

Most people can stay motivated for two or three months. A few people can stay motivated for thirty years—or as long as it takes to win. Hire these immediately and promote them quickly.

—FRANK VIZZARE

One person can be an island of excellence in a sea of mediocrity.

—STEPHEN R. COVEY

You can't just sit down and say, "Okay, I made a difference today, I'm done." I wake up every day thinking, "What else can I do to make a difference, not only for myself but for others?"

—ANDREA JAEGER

The drive for excellence assures excitement!

—ROBERT SCHULLER

Customers can smell emotional commitment a mile away. Every single person in the entire organization needs to speak the language of quality and service very fluently.

—TOM PETERS

"Satisfied" customers isn't good enough anymore—you have to create raving fans!

—JON MAY

Better quality + lesser price = value + spiritual attitude of our employees = unbeatable.

—HERB KELLEHER

Remember when you were at your best? Now be there again!

—ANDREW MEAD

When people say they are committed, they don't say that we "hope" to win, or it would sure be "nice" to win, or we "wouldn't mind" winning. They say, and they mean, that they fully expect to win.

—DON WARD

At the end of the year, who wants to hear, "We almost had a great year. We almost achieved our goals. We almost met our projections." Instead, let's look each other in the eye and say, "We did."

—DAN ZADRA

Who are the most important people in the company? Everyone.

—PETE SELLECK

Also available from The Gift of Inspiration Series:

Be Happy.
Remember to Live, Love,
Laugh and Learn.

Be the Difference

Because of You™
Celebrating the Difference
You Make™

Brilliance™
Uncommon Voices From
Uncommon Women™

Commitment to Excellence™
Celebrating the Very Best

Expect Success

Forever Remembered™
A Gift for the Grieving Heart™

I Believe in You™
To your heart, your dream and
the difference you make.

Little Miracles™
To renew your dreams,
lift your spirits, and strengthen
your resolve™

Reach for the Stars™
Give up the Good to Go
for the Great.

Thank You
In appreciation of you,
and all that you do.

To Your Success™
Thoughts to Give Wings to
Your Work and Your Dreams™

Together We Can™
Celebrating the power of
a team and a dream™

Whatever It Takes™
A Journey into the Heart
of Human Achievement™

You've Got a Friend™
Thoughts to Celebrate
the Joy of Friendship™